Green Notebook,
Winter Road

ALSO BY JANE COOPER

Scaffolding: Selected Poems (1984, 1993)
Maps & Windows (1974)
The Weather of Six Mornings (1969)

JANE
COOPER

Green Notebook,
Winter Road

Tilbury House, Publishers
Gardiner, Maine

Tilbury House, Publishers
132 Water Street
Gardiner, ME 04345

First Printing

Library of Congress Cataloging-in-Publication Data

Cooper, Jane, 1924-
        Green notebook, winter road / Jane Cooper
                p.   cm.
        ISBN 0-88448-141-7 : $19.95. ISBN 0-88448-142-5 : $12.95.
        1. Women--Poetry.   I. Title.
        PS3553. 059G74   1994
        811 ' .54--dc20   94-4867
                                                                             CIP

Design: Edith Allard
Production: Mark Melnicove and Lisa Reece
Printing (cover and jacket): John Pow Co., Boston, Massachusetts
Printing (text) and binding: Vail-Ballou, Binghamton, New York
Cover photo: Padma Hejmadi

For Sally Appleton Weber
and in honor of Muriel Rukeyser
and Shirley Eliason Haupt

My friends are my "estate"
— E.D. to Samuel Bowles, 1858?

CONTENTS

Green Notebook,
Winter Road

I.

ON THE EDGE OF THE MOMENT

The Green Notebook

There are 64 panes in each window of the Harrisville church
where we sit listening to a late Haydn quartet. Near the ceiling clouds
build up, slowly brightening, then disperse, till the evening sky
glistens like the pink inside of a shell over uncropped grass,
over a few slant graves.

At Sargent Pond the hollows are the color of strong tea.
Looking down you can see decomposed weeds and the muscular bronze and
          green
stems of some water lilies. Out there on the float
three figures hang between water and air, the heat breathes them, they no
          longer speak.
It is a seamless July afternoon.

Nameless. Slowly gathering. . . . It seems I am on the edge
of discovering the green notebook containing all the poems of my life,
I mean the ones I never wrote. The meadow turns intensely green.
The notebook is under my fingers. I read. My companions read.
Now thunder joins in, scurry of leaves. . . .

Ordinary Detail

I'm trying to write a poem that will alert me to my real life,
a poem written in the natural speech of the breakfast table,
of a girl spooning yogurt, pausing, the spoon held aloft
while she gestures toward the exact next turning of her thought.

It would have to be a poem dense with ordinary detail
the way the sun, spilling across walnut and balled-up napkins,
can pick out cups, plates, the letter from which someone has just read aloud,
with evenhanded curiosity, leaving behind a gloss of pleasure.

And yet this poem too must allow for the unseen.
Last night the girl dreamed of a triple-locked door
at the head of a short flight of steps. Why couldn't she get in?
How to take possession of that room? Will it be hers to keep?

Remembering, she loses track of her sentence, frowns suddenly, smiles,
excusing herself to the others. A friend's brother died of AIDS.
Sensuality is not the secret; it's more like redemption, or violence. . . .
The girl is walking furiously, under a mild, polluted sky.

My friend

Sylvia said: *When I was younger —*
you know how in the work of most composers
a single line dominates, the melody line? —
Well, years ago I'd think only about my daughter
or only about my marriage, about how to sing,
what Freud meant or some friend. . . . But in Bach,
every voice is equal, each line has invention.
That's how it is for me now, life and death are equal,
I'm neither going up the hill nor down. . . .

She paused, then extended her fingers
like Landowska addressing the keyboard. *But I don't know,* she broke off,
whether I'm making myself clear. . . .

My Mother in Three Acts

At the top of the hill you were Muriel,
pale but still powerful as a Sumo wrestler,
generous, mother of mysteries held in reserve.
You were already dead then; I knew I couldn't save you.
In the nursery school room I began to rearrange
brightly colored clay figures: *la Sagrada Familia.*

Tripping down the hill you were Betty,
blond and still fashionable but too thin,
needling me, cosseting me. Dying of cancer
only sharpened your wit. I knew I couldn't save you —
I could barely even keep up! Mother of the quick retort,
of the enchanting story, mother of gifts and dissatisfactions.

At the bottom of the hill just as we reached the
house I had rented, I glimpsed a fugitive girl,
face turned aside toward the woods, slipping away
in a seagreen Japanese kimono; her hair was brown.
Was it you, mother of boyishness, mother of
deception, who saved me once, the one who evades me still?

What the Seer Said

She said I would see the future,
that is to say, my father,
through an ophthalmologic device.

That man was no good, she warned,
but I persisted: *No one,
no one has done me any harm.*

The machine moved on silent wheels.
She fastened my eyes to two wells.
I was pasted to the deep.

The first image was of jangling
kaleidoscopic angles;
the second, inchoate dark.

From a constricted throat
I brought a few words: *My father
was a generous man — but remote.*

At *remote* the darkness unveiled
a mist-becalmed lake and pale
sky and hills like loaves —

blue on blue on blue,
undramatic, unconfused
as the fan of Ma Yüan —

So this was my father's house!
this courteous, ancestral place!
I lifted my eyes, in relief,

and tasted the mortal cold.
I sat down by the water's edge, old,
deprived, at home, at peace.

Estrangement

You dream someone is leaving you, though he says kindly, *It's not that you're cold*
or *After all you're an affectionate person.*

You can't explain how hard it is to explain or even to write this poem
so you blurt, *I was ashamed, they put me in the class for remedial speech.*

The doctor leans forward: *Do you feel you have failed me recently?*
The dream answers through you: *I am locked in a struggle with the truth.*

(I was ashamed, I couldn't speak, they voted me out of the shelter.
Like Rousseau's Sleeping Gypsy I lay exposed to the nuclear night
till a dog found my throat.)

You watch your own back growing smaller up the beach.

Long, Disconsolate Lines

in memory of Shirley Eliason Haupt

Because it is a gray day but not snowy, because traffic grinds by outside,
because I woke myself crying *help!* to no other in my bed and no god,
because I am in confusion about god,
because the tree out there with its gray, bare limbs is shaped like a lyre,
but it is only January, nothing plays it, no lacerating March sleet,
no thrum of returning rain,
because its arms are empty of buds or even of protective snow,
I am in confusion, words harbor in my throat, I hear not one confident tune,
and however long I draw out this sentence
it will not arrive at any truth.

It's true my friend died in September and I have not yet begun to mourn.
Overnight, without warning, the good adversary knocked at her door,
the one she so often portrayed
as a cloud-filled drop out the cave's mouth, crumpled dark of an old garden
        chair. . . .
But a lyre-shaped tree? yes, a lyre-shaped tree. It's true that at twenty-four
in the dripping, raw Iowa woods
she sketched just such a tree, and I saw it, fell in love with its half-heard lament
as if my friend, in her pristine skin, already thrashed by the storm-blows ahead,
had folded herself around them,
as if she gave up nothing, as if she sang.

Bloodroot

Reading your words
to find they are
just your words. . . .

Waking:
what is this heaviness? only
a matter of money, or closure. Oh yes, the lease,
the rent is going up.

During the war
how I shouted at my mother:
It's only a thing! A thing got broken, suppose
some friend had been killed!

Reading your words.
Remembering how we were friends
in, say, 1974.

Fifteen years ago now, and the whole body
changes, every living cell,
in seven years, and seven years,

and now this one:
fragile as bloodroot,

releasing its unhurried freshness,
half earth, half air.

The Calling

All the voices of the sea called *Muriel!*
Muriel from the Irish *Muirgheal,* meaning
muir, sea, plus *gel,* bright, or in Old English
pure, clean, from the Greek for eyeball

> You who equated *women, ships, lost voices,*
> who lost your speech, then your clear vision,
> who loved flying, sailing, drove a fast car
> with the calm of a centaur, lost your gangrenous toe

from *mori,* body of water, root of Old English *mere,*
a pond or possibly mermaid

> You whose erect carriage was like a figurehead's,
> who lay down outside the Senate, stood by the Korean jail,
> dropped once at a reading of Smart's "Rejoice in the Lamb"
> like a tree felled in the church

whence our cognates *cormorant,*
ultramarine

> Now I perceive what the calling is
> here by this estuary,
> I a year younger than you were when you died

> Body of brightness! I trace your undulant tones
> tossed on a clearing wind

> whose last, next book was to be FINDINGS
> whose magnified eye stares out past Hariot's trail,
> who crossed out *to,* wrote *from*

I a lost voice
moving, calling you
on the edge of the moment that is now the center.
~~To~~ From the open sea

II.
FAMILY STORIES

Hotel de Dream

Justice-keepers! justice-keepers! for
Muriel Rukeyser and James Wright

Suppose we could telephone the dead.
Muriel, I'd say, can you hear me?
Jim, can you talk again?

And I'd begin to tell them the stories they loved to hear:
how my father, as a young boy, watched Cora Crane
parade through the streets of Jacksonville with her girls
in an open barouche with silver fittings;
how the bay haunches gleamed as they twitched off flies,
polished hooves fetched down smartly into the dust,
ostrich feathers tickled the palates of passers-by.

Muriel, I'd say, shall we swing along Hudson Street
underneath the highway and walk out together on the docks?

. . . the river would be glittering, my grandmother
would be bargaining
with a black man on a dock in Jacksonville;
grapefruit and oranges would be piled up like cannonballs
at the fort in Old St. Augustine . . .

I'll never put you in a nursing home, you said early that year,
I promise, Jane, I'll never put you in a nursing home.

Later Cora Crane showed her dogs right next to my aunt's.
They had a good conversation about bloodlines
amidst the clean smells of kennel shavings and well-brushed dog
but never, of course, met socially
although she had dined with Henry James.

Jim, I'd say, remember that old poem "The Faithful"
you helped me by caring for? how what we owe to the dead
is to go on living? More than ever
I want to go on living.

15

But now you have become part of it, friends of my choosing years,
friends whose magnificent voices
will reverberate always, if only through machines,
tell me how to redress the past,
how to relish yet redress
my sensuous, precious, upper-class,
unjust white child's past.

From the Journal Concerning My Father

1

It all started with the maps. Hanging in the living room, the hall, on the way up the stairs, were the old maps of Florida, the flowery land. One showed an Indian woman carrying her child, one showed beavers building a dam and all the plantation sites around Charleston, one showed the round world colored yellow and blue and had been drawn only three years after the great voyage of Magellan. One dull black and white map, a government document, showed Fort Cooper, an outpost in the Seminole Wars.

And then there were the family stories. My father's grandfather, that fierce and unrelenting man, told my father about sailing around Cape Horn in a clipper ship, on his way to the Gold Rush, and how he had come back penniless on the back of a burro right across the Isthmus of Panamá. Even before that his mother had sent him to Spain to trace the genealogy of her family in the Royal Libraries of Seville. My father's grandfather maintained that the true history of Florida would never be written till the royal archives could be opened and transcribed.

He disowned his first-born son — one of two who survived to manhood — for doing the honorable thing and marrying a Minorcan fisherman's daughter, from St. Augustine. The Spaniards had looked down on the Minorcans, because some had the blood of slaves. Great-Uncle Charlie was in Congress, till he broke with his party over Free Silver.

Even in my father's boyhood they still kept Spanish hours in Florida. His grandfather unlocked the doors to his law office at seven every morning, came home for the big dinner of the day at one, took his siesta, then returned to the office from four or five until eight. At nine he presided over (but did not share in) a cold supper. Often the whole family would sit out on the porch afterwards with newspapers wrapped around their ankles to keep off the mosquitoes, enjoying the cool of the evening. Probably he wore a white linen suit, and on the way to the office a fine Panamá hat, and smoked Havana cigars. His sons would take off their hats to him in the street and bow but, preoccupied, he would not recognize them.

My young father slept with a loaded pistol under his pillow every night, such was the incidence of crime in Jacksonville.

Uncle Merian believed America had never paid back her debt to Kosciusko. After the War To End Wars, he flew for Poland, strafing from his single-engine plane the toy bands of Russian cavalry. Then he was in Russian prison camp, starving for bread and books. Later he dined with Haile Selassie, in Abyssinia, whose warriors still wore chain mail. In Persia he crossed mountains higher than the Alps on foot, with the Bakhtiari, to find grass for their flocks. His was the first team to film an elephant stampede from underneath. With all his heart he believed that film would revolutionize the study of anthropology. At home we read about his exploits in *Asia* Magazine or *The National Geographic* — back copies kept in the chest at the turn of the stairs in my grandmother's tall, quiet house — or pored over occasional postcards. One postcard showed him squinting into the sun from under his pale topi hat, the white gibbon ape on his shoulder.

He had not yet dreamed of King Kong.

At home, my father seemed the steady older brother, genius of music and gardens. As a boy he had built a boat on my grandmother's veranda and launched it one day with his best friend on the St. John's River, just down the end of the block. Taking along my ten-year-old aunt as crew, they set sail down the Inland Waterway for a weeklong trip. As a lawyer he drove constantly up and down the state in his old Model A. But on Sundays he dug in the flowerbeds; restlessly, he moved the japonica bush, which consequently never bloomed. I would stand beside him sometimes, gazing out at the river, smelling the good smell of turned earth. Below the bluff he kept chickens, ducks, guinea fowl. He loved exotic birds and showed them at the Florida state fair. He was a ham radio operator, and we listened to Lily Pons, with her high, thread-like voice, all the way from New York, by some miracle of the short wave.

It was he who collected the maps.

2

Live oak or magnolia, I rarely looked up at the leaves but only felt their cave-like shade and something like rope burn on the insides of my thighs. Gazing out at water or air, often I would sit astride. Below me the exposed root plunged over the bluff toward the river and halfway down buried itself again in earth. On the last day we lived in that place, I slipped away to say goodbye to the tree. I lay along the root full length and tried to breathe into my own body its peaceful, tidal pulse. From a great way off I heard a trunk lid slam, my mother's voice. . . .

Goodbye! Goodbye to the river, to the sentinel tree that seemed to measure the depth of the sky! A procession of ants of the same rusty black or eggplant color began to circumnavigate the bark just below my wrist. Goodbye to the umbilical root that for nine years had fastened me to this earth!

the earth that is nowhere
that is the true home

3

Earth-spirit, wood-spirit, stone,
father, Other, exposed root
I said goodbye to by the river, where
are you now? I fondle a glass eye.

The eye reflects leaves, stars,
galaxies. . . . Space
was always my demon, the unreachable.
From a black hole, a wavering
flute song, readable.

4

In 1935 he told his new friend, the professor of music — gazing short-sightedly out across his new flowerbeds — that soon there would be regular commercial air travel to Europe and the Orient.

He flew all over Ireland with Lindbergh, in a two-seater plane, to pick out the very best site — at Foynes, near the mouth of the Shannon — for the new airport.

He was delighted to discover, on President DeValera's desk, when he called to negotiate landing rights, a volume of poems by Father Flynn, his grandmother's favorite, who had been the Sweet Singer of the Confederacy.

In 1940 he explained to my brother that the United States had never engaged in a war in which someone bearing the family name had not taken part.

He saw in Vietnam the beginning of a long imperial decline.

When in 1965 I asked him to write something about his family for the grandchildren, he replied: "When I was a boy in the South, after Reconstruction, you had to choose whether to spend your life going forward or looking back. I have never looked back."

My father said Law should precede Man into Space.

He said the circumference of the earth was too small for intelligent aircraft design or navigation.

In 1951, before Sputnik, he said we must decide the legal limits of the upper air. At what point does the atmosphere grow so thin that the concept of national sovereignty becomes meaningless?

Did he die still hoping that human justice could precede technology into the uncharted silences that had terrified Pascal?

Childhood in Jacksonville, Florida

What is happening to me now that loved faces
are beginning to float free of their names
like a tide of balloons, while a dark street
wide enough only for carriages, in a familiar city,
loses itself
to become South America?

Oh I am the last member of the nineteenth century!
And my excitement about sex, which was not of today,
is diffusing itself in generosity of mind.

For my mind is relaxing its grip, and a fume
of antique telephones, keys, fountain pens, torn roadmaps,
old stories of the way Nan Powell died
(poor girl!) rises in the air
detached but accurate —
almost as accurate
as if I'd invented them.

Welcome then, poverty!
flights of strings above the orange trees!

The Hobby Lobby

A stalwart country woman
in a clean, flowered smock, she explained
how she would get up before sunrise

in Tennessee to gather
cobwebs at first light.
How, as if layering a poultice,

she mashed them together, still dewy;
they made a sort of rug,
gray, slightly elastic.

Cobwebs are famous healers
if you mash them into a cut
but hers became spongy beds

for 2-inch-square watercolors
done with the tiniest brush.
The crowd seemed alert, not bored.

The paintings were certainly novel!
mountains, sunsets, cows
in colors coagulated —

My mother gave an odd shudder.
Imagine July, then August,
in Flushing Meadows, *talking.*

My father's second cousin
(once removed) went on with her spiel.
She didn't recognize us

or did she? Mother worried
all the way home on the train.
My father might not *say,*

but they had more in common than blood:
she had made it to the Hobby Lobby
of the 1939 World's Fair.

Class

How the shrimp fisherman's daughter did a handstand against the schoolyard
       fence
proving she owned no drawers
just as my grandmother's old black Packard drove up like a hearse

How we dug in the woods for pirate gold
and found only the bootleggers' empties

Wanda's Blues

Ortega Public School, 1932

Wanda's daddy was a railroadman, she was his little wife.
Ernest's sister had a baby, she was nobody's wife.
Wanda was the name and wandering, wandering was their way of life.

Ernest's sister was thirteen, too old for school anyway.
When Ernest couldn't pass third grade, they kept him there anyway,
hunched up tight in a littler kid's desk with his hair sticking out like hay.

But Wanda was small and clean as a cat, she gave nothing away.

At school the plate lunch cost ten cents, milk was a nickel more.
Shrimps were selling for a nickel a pound — those shrimpers' kids were real
      poor,
they lived in an abandoned army camp, the bus dropped them off at the door.

Gossip in the schoolyard had it that Wanda swept and sewed
and cooked the supper for her daddy when he wasn't on the road.
She never told where she ate or she slept, how she did her lessons, if she had an
      ol' lamp. . . .
That wasn't the traveling man's code.

Wanda was smart and watchful, we let her into our games.
Wanda always caught on quick whether it was long division or games.
She never gave a thing away except for her lingering name.

I would say it over: *Wanda   Wanda*

April, and school closed early. We never saw her again.
Her daddy loved an empty freight, he must have lit out again.
Wanda-a-a-a the steam whistle hollered. O my American refrain!

The Past

It seemed, when I was a child, as if you could just reach back and rummage in the 19th century. For instance the ear doctor took me on his knee and later my mother said, *His uncle fought in the War of 1812.* How could that be? It was 1929. And his father had been a famous general for the Confederacy. Then there was Cousin Josiah, U. S. Congress, Retired. He told my mother never to trust anyone who said he had grown up before stoves unless he could tell you how to turn a flapjack. The correct way (in Cousin Josiah's house they were still cooking at the great open fireplace until he was 17) is to pour the batter out along the scorching hearth, wait till the edges begin to curl, slide a greased string underneath, and Flip! Cousin Josiah also told of two ancient people of color who had been born on the family place — once a plantation — in Delaware. *All they knew* was (in the old man's case) how to plant and ret and comb flax, and (in the old woman's) how to spin it. Every year she wove not much more than a single linen handkerchief. They had never been man and wife, nor were they sister and brother, but Cousin Josiah hoped they could die in the same winter, as they had lived. His son was a Quaker witness, whose safeconduct from the Gestapo meant he could enter any prison in Paris during the Nazi Occupation.

How have we come so far? How did we live through (in the persons, for me, of my father, of my uncle) radio, aviation, film, the conquest through exploration of Equatorial Africa, Persia, and Siam? My father thought the moon-walk silly, there were more promising worlds.

And how do I connect in my own body — that is, through touch — the War of 1812 with the smart rocket nosing its way via CNN down a Baghdad street? How much can two arms hold? How soon will my body, which already contains a couple of centuries, become almost transparent and begin to shiver apart?

Being Southern

1

It's like being German.
Either you remember that yours was the defeated country
(The South breeds the finest soldiers, my uncle said,
himself a general in one of his incarnations)
or you acknowledge the guilt, not even your own guilt, but

Can any white person write this, whose ancestors once kept slaves?

2

Of course there were "good" Germans.

My father was still under 30, a passionate Wilsonian, when he was named a delegate to the 1916 Democratic Convention. By the end of the first evening he had discovered that eleven of the other Florida delegates were members of the Klan, he couldn't answer for the twelfth, he was number 13.

Only a few years later he argued for, and won, token black representation on the Jacksonville school board.

And my aunt as a girl went into the sweatshops to interview Cuban cigar workers, all women. She founded the first Girl Scout troop in the South for, as she put it, *colored children.* True, it was segregated. But it was the first.

Take your guilt to school. Read your guilt in your diplomas or the lines of the marriage ceremony. Face your guilt head-on in the eyes of lover, neighbor, child. Ask to be buried in your guilt.

Of course they were paternalistic. I honor their accomplishments. What more have I ever done?

When is memory transforming? when, a form of real estate?

3

Transplanted "north" in 1934 I never questioned
a town that received its distinguished refugees
with a mix of pride and condescension: the specialist in Christian iconography
in her man-tailored suits, Einstein *like a disembodied spirit*
pacing our leafy sidewalks. Only because my best friend lived next door
would I glimpse him, sometimes at twilight, tuning his violin
as his back yard filled up with tents

But why can't I remember the actual men and women who slept in those tents,
among patches of ragged tigerlilies? the children with skinny arms, who would
soon be passed along. . . ?

All he could vouch for. Not famous. At their backs
the six million.

Seventeen Questions About KING KONG

The most amazing thing I know about Jane
Cooper is that she's the niece of King Kong
— James Wright

Is it a myth? And if so, what does it tell us about ourselves?

Is Kong a giant ape, or is he an African, beating his chest like a responsive gong?

Fay Wray lies in the hand of Kong as in the hand of God the Destroyer. She gives the famous scream. Is the final conflict (as Merian C. Cooper maintained) really between man and the forces of nature, or is it a struggle for the soul and body of the white woman?

Who was more afraid of the dark, Uncle Merian or his older sister? She was always ready to venture downstairs whenever he heard a burglar.

When he was six his Confederate uncle gave him EXPLORATIONS AND ADVENTURES IN EQUATORIAL AFRICA by Paul du Chaillu, 1861. Does that island of prehistoric life forms still rise somewhere off the coast of the Dark Continent, or is it lost in preconscious memory?

Is fear of the dark the same as fear of sexuality? Mary Coldwell his mother would have destroyed herself had she not been bound by a thread to the wrist of her wakeful nurse. What nights theirs must have been!

Why was I too first called after Mary (or Merian) Coldwell, till my mother, on the morning of the christening, decided it was a hard-luck name?

How does our rising terror at so much violence, as Kong drops the sailors one by one into the void or rips them with his fangs, resolve itself into shame at Kong's betrayal?

Is Kong's violence finally justified, because he was in chains?

Is King Kong our Christ?

Watch him overturn the el-train, rampage through the streets! But why is New York, the technological marvel, so distrusted, when technologically the film was unsurpassed for its time?

Must the anthropologist always dream animal dreams? Must we?

Kong clings to the thread of the Empire State Building. He wavers. Why did Uncle Merian and his partner Schoedsack choose to play the airmen who over and over exult to shoot Kong down?

He said: *Why did I ever leave Africa?* — and then as if someone had just passed a washcloth over his face: *But I've had a very good marriage.*

Clementene

1

I always thought she was white, I thought she was an Indian
because of her high-bridged nose, coin-perfect profile
where she sat in an upstairs window, turning sheets sides-to-the-middle —
There are so many things wrong with this story,
Muriel, *I could not tell you* —

Her cheeks were oddly freckled, and her hair would be squeezed down
into a compact, small knot at the nape, gray as chicken wire, gray
as the light, unaffectionate glance her eyes would give
if she lifted them from her work.
No child would interrupt her.

She came twice a year to do the sewing, she slept in the house,
but her meals were brought up, so that she dined by the Singer,
now and then staring fixedly across the river. She joined neither white
in the dining room nor colored in the kitchen.
Her wishes were respected.

Later I saw the same light, disconcerting gaze and futuristic planes
in Oppenheimer's face, but she looked most like my grandmother's friend Miss
        Gertrude
who taught me to tat. Once we moved north, Mother confided
of the *two finest families* in Jacksonville, no one could be sure
whose father was her father.

2

Muriel, I never told you, I never revealed how Clementene
died in our house a white woman and was claimed by her black daughter.

How she *flung up her arms* in wild grief
so different from Clementene's reserve.

How she *hollered and called on Christ Jesus,*
flinging her body from side to side at the foot of the staircase.

How the police arrived, it was nine o'clock at night,
long past my bedtime.

How I leaned over the stair rail,
unnoticed for once, as their torches burst in.

It seemed as if tumultuous shadows
crawled through the door, odors of pinestraw, magnolia, river bottom —

They are carrying a blanketed stretcher.
Now the daughter follows, still whimpering into my mother's small-boned
       shoulder.

I had seen how a mother could be mourned.
Now I watch my mother shiver and pull away.

Why, if I was not an accomplice,
did I feel — do I feel still — this complex shame?

How Can I Speak for Her?

First there is my little grandfather, I think he is no more than four or five. Anyway it must be after the War, and after his twin brother, his only sister, and his mother have all perished in one of the yellow fever epidemics that swept the low countries of Georgia and South Carolina in the wake of Sherman's march. He is living with his grandmother, the "Castilian." And where is his stiff-necked father, lately of the Confederate Treasury, who once rounded Cape Horn in a clipper ship and returned from California on muleback, right across the Isthmus of Panamá, but was deemed too frail to bear arms? Once, famously, he had nursed the sick and dying in Savannah, but his own young wife he could not save. Once already, through overstrain, he had entirely lost his speech. Is he still head of the Southern Masonic Female College, or ("his health failing") has he departed for Florida, where (but it is Reconstruction?) he will serve in the first postwar legislature of that violent and rudimentary state?

I believe it is Athens, Georgia, I believe it must be Jacksonville; either way I imagine an ill-painted house on a swept street somewhere near the outskirts of town. But of course I don't know where they lived really, I only know my grandfather is playing on the porch at his grandmother's feet. Maybe she is in a rocking chair, mending. In front of them stretches the dusty street, parched white by the sun, empty even of animals. I would like to imagine a sleeping dog, whose neck skin twitches as he dreams, or a chicken or two pecking in the dirt — but probably there are no chickens left, in this summer when so much has already been eaten or long since carried away.

What follows now is confused — but after all there is no film-maker here, to concentrate the image not only in space and light but also in time, and speculation. Down the street limps an old black woman, a woman nobody knows (in this town where everybody, black or white, is acquainted with everyone else). I think she must be complaining a bit, or singing, just under her breath. Has she finally limped away from some burned plantation where she was a slave for forty-odd years, having refused to leave earlier? And if so, where does she live now? Never mind, she has certainly not passed this way before, along this particular road, at just this hour when my great-great-grandmother chances to look up from her shaded and peeling porch. But she must live somewhere nearby, for from this day forward she will come every week, limping through sun and rain, till one of the two old women dies.

So what does my little grandfather see, as he too lifts his eyes from his imaginary wars, where with unfailing regularity the twigs called Yankees are beaten back by the brave twigs called Confederates? Perhaps it is no surprise to him that the stranger is of a peculiarly deep, unmixed black color, that her face is shining but scarred, that she wears a clean headrag with ample, nodding wings above her bleached-out, worn slave dress. Later, certain white people would say the "best" slaves came from the Guinea Coast, and my grandfather would say that if the South had just been let alone, of course the slaves would soon have been freed, slavery being un-Christian and also against the natural law. But at four or five, I think he hardly scans the new arrival. Had she been a chicken, he would have noticed her.

His grandmother starts up from her chair — now *that* is a surprise, this woman whose severity and composure are almost never shaken, who cradles the newborn and the dying with even-handed skill. Who lost her own mother at eight, her father at fourteen, who was immediately married off for propriety's sake, who followed her North American husband from the home plantation in Cuba to the rougher hills of Georgia, who with her surviving children followed him again to flat, malarial north Florida (always the destination must have seemed wilder, more poverty-stricken and remote), only to refugee back, a widow, right into the path of Sherman's troops. Who years ago had sent her eldest son, the frail one, to find out the history of her family in the Royal Libraries of Seville. Who called herself Castilian, though she was almost certainly half French, and would live to scold my little grandfather for the miserable accent with which he spoke any foreign language they attempted to teach him at school. . . . Am I doing her justice, I wonder? this exile who, often hungry herself now, must provide not only food but the will to live for her son's defenseless sons? How much is fact, how much fond family embroidery? The one thing that is clear, that has come down without question through five generations — splendid or chilling, depending on the tale-teller, incomprehensible or simply necessary, depending on your receipt for survival — is her pride.

Slave-mistress from childhood, when the women ran the plantations. Familiar, since childhood, with the lost markings of at least two tribes. . . .

What my grandfather remembered, all those many years later, was that she called out in a language none of them knew she knew, a language no one had heard her speak before, from so deep in her throat it was as if she coughed up stones. That she flew down the steps to stop just short of the African in the dust. That slowly then, as if unsure, she just traced the scarifications graved like a cat's face into the African face. That each met the gaze of the last person with whom she could converse. That — but how can I speak for her, whose name would again be lost? — they embraced.

III.
GIVE US THIS DAY

_____

The Infusion Room

1

Mercy on Maryanne who through a hole beneath her collarbone drinks the
        life-preserving fluid, while in her arm
another IV tube drips something green. "It never affects me," she says, "I'm
        fortunate."
She has Crohn's and rheumatoid arthritis and now osteoporosis, as well as no
        gamma globulin
as we all have no gamma globulin, or at least not enough. Mercy on Aaron,
her son, who at fifteen has Hodgkins and arthritis and no gamma globulin,
        who is out of school
just for the moment. "He's so bright," the doctor says, "he'll make it up." But
        of course
you never (as I remember) quite make it up. (Sitting up all night so as not to
        cough,
coughing so hard I tore the cartilage off three ribs. "If I was God," the then-
        doctor said,
"I'd design better ribs.")

Mercy on Mitzi who shook for three hours the first day I was there, and
        Cynthia
who cried because of the pain in her legs but aspires to horseback riding.
"Mitzi's tough," the nurse said admiringly, and I thought, could I ever be so
        tough?
Could I wear a velvet cap like Cynthia? Mitzi's on chemo.

And mercy on Paul, who drives a cab part-time and has sores on his ankles.
"If you could put your feet up more," the doctor suggests. He winces as she
        touches his skin, explains
if he could just finish college he could get a better job, but to finish college he
        has to drive this cab,
and I think of my luck all those years teaching at a college, the flexible hours,
        pleasant rooms
where you could always put your feet up if need be. Mercy on Mike,
the pilot, who looks like a jockey, who shows us pictures of his 14-month-old
        girl,

who used to be allergic, as I am allergic, so that now while Mike reads the
  comics,
his friend leans against the wall, thumbing a computer manual, faithful, a tad
  overweight.
Mercy on the wholesale grocer, the man who sells prostheses, the used-Caddy
  salesman moving to glossy Florida,
the one who says candidly, "The first two days of each week are OK, then I
  begin to get tired."

Mercy on the black kid strapped to his Walkman, mercy on all like him who
  fall asleep.
Mercy on Sally Jessy Raphael and the interminable talk show flickering down
  the morning as we drift, or shiver, or sleep.
Aaron puts his huge sneakers up on Maryanne's seat and she holds his hand
  lightly while he sleeps;
they look like the Creation of Adam.

2

I think if you could see us now we'd resemble giant grasshoppers
whose skinny elbows vibrate slightly above their heads, or I think that the room

if you approached it by space ship would look like a busy harbor,
crammed with barges, their curious cargo, and cranes extended or at half mast,

but all functional, needed. The TV twitters. The nurses are taking a break
from the hard business of giving us each day (at two- or three- or four-week
  intervals)

our daily, habitable lives. We too could go on a talk show,
challenging truckers' wives, twins who have lost their Other. I peel open my
  sandwich

with my good, unencumbered right hand. The IV poles gleam, we float on our
  black recliners.
It is almost time for the soaps.

The Children's Ward

1

Nanny was Irish, I told my mother, *born* in Scotland. Her sister was Head of Ladies' Ready To Wear at the biggest shop in Greenoch. Her oldest sister that was, there were nine in the family. The youngest of all was Our Joseph, not much older than me, and when the little princesses visited Greenoch, Nanny went to see them, along with all the other people lining the streets, but they couldn't hold a candle to Our Joseph. Nanny took care of me because once before she had taken care of a little boy who was sick the same way I was. So she understood my diet. "Poor wee thing," she would say and tell how one day somebody brought her a box of chocolates and the boy took some, which of course he wasn't supposed to do, and when he heard her coming he sat down on the box and squashed the chocolates flat. But when she caught me lifting icing off my sister's birthday cake, I was spanked. "This hurts me more than it does you," Nanny would say, her wrists like steel, while I screamed. Yet she looked back on that boy with tenderness. "Poor wee lamb" — and she explained how with the disease we had you were supposed to die before you were seven. "And did he die, Nanny? Is he dead now?" But I never found out.

Curds without whey — four times a day Nanny put the junket through the ricer and squeezed it dry — bananas, the lean of bacon, protein milk that tasted like chalk. I was standing holding up my glass and crying. I cried all the time now, every morning playing with the other children I would start to cry. My grandmother's stylish heels clicked across the floor. "Here Junebug, it's not as bad as all that, I'll show you." She took a gulp, puckered up her lips and rushed out into the hall. Nanny handed the glass back to me. "Drink up," she said, out of patience. "If you don't drink your milk like a good girl, we'll be planting daisies on your grave by August."

There was a woman in their town who lost all five sons in the War, and when the Armistice came and they had the big parade, she closed her window shades and refused to watch. I imagined how that house looked, small, between two taller houses, with black shades. I liked the stories about Our Joseph better. And how they all slept together in the one big bed. I used to wake up early and see Nanny lying in the other half of our bed, her nose pointing to the ceiling, her firm chest rising and falling under the saint's medal and small gold cross. "When Father says *turn*," she would command, "we all turn."

God knew Nanny would have saved my life if she could, but since there was apparently no saving it, she did her duty. Her duty was to see I didn't die any sooner than I had to and make sure I got to Heaven when I did die. So I had A CHILD'S TALES FROM THE BIBLE, in red and gold, every night and "The Catholic Hour" over the radio on Sundays. All day I looked forward to bedtime. My favorite was Moses in the Bulrushes. Fancy finding a live baby floating in a nest down our river, the way Pharaoh's Daughter had! But I hated Abraham. In the picture he held the knife over Isaac's head and Isaac looked terrified; the ram bleated in the bushes. When I had been really sick, lying on my back in bed with a swollen stomach, someone brought Harriet to visit me. Harriet was three, a year younger than me. Over the curve of my huge stomach, I could just see her wedged between the foot of the bed and the wall. She was carrying a present for me but was too scared to budge. After she had gone Nanny said, "Harriet's a Jew." "What's a Jew?" I said. "They're God's chosen people." A few days later I announced, "I'm going to be a Jew." "You can't" — Nanny stopped folding — "you have to be born one." "Can't I ever?" I thought about Harriet's curls and dark, reproachful eyes. She was the most beautiful child I had ever seen. I wanted to be chosen more than anything.

"You have to learn to read now you're five because I learned to read when I was five," said Isabel importantly. I was squeezed into the old highchair because I liked looking down on things; no one used it any more. "No, I don't," I said, "nobody has to learn to read till they're six." At eight, Pen was still learning. Besides, I didn't want to keep growing older this way. The other children raced up and down the room. Nanny burst in, her hands still red from the soapsuds. "There," she declared, plucking me out of the highchair, "can't you see you've gone and made Jane cry again?" "I didn't, I didn't," protested Isabel, "you're unfair." "Don't be impertinent," said Nanny — she pronounced it im*pair*tinent. In her arms I was crying harder, leaning my head into her white, starched shoulder. Pen and Isabel must hate me. Even when the circus came to town, on its way north from winter quarters, they might not get to go for fear they'd bring home another germ.

But the first night I got sick Pen had been excited. We were in our small summer house then, where I used to stand up in my crib to watch the mountains and the long black freight train hooted out of its tunnel in the clear evening light. I was perched on the toilet; a bare light bulb burned against the wall. Pen danced across the bathroom, shrieking and laughing. "There goes the King!" he shrieked. "There goes the Queen!" That was an old game we had, whenever a bad thunderstorm hit. Pen played chess, and he liked to pretend the thunder was giant chessmen falling off the board of Heaven and rolling around on the ground. But tonight the thunder was my farts. Bent over on the toilet seat, queasy and trembling, I hurt with laughter because of Pen. My brother's wiry body flashed by. A shadow jerked up the wall. "There goes the Queen!" I shouted wildly. "There goes a pawn!"

Then I was lying in bed with my stomach puffed so high I couldn't bear to sit up even against pillows. I hurt all the time. My mother read THE WATER BABIES. Every time she got to the last page and shut the book I would demand to hear it over again, right from the beginning. Poor Tom, dirty and miserable, sank underneath the river and the whole husk of his body was washed away, and soon he was clean and shining, no bigger than Daddy's thumb. My father blocked the light in the bedroom door. We stared at each other. Then the doorway was empty, he had left without saying anything. "He can't stand to see anybody sick," said my mother to my aunt, in a voice I wasn't supposed to catch. My aunt began to sing to me so my mother could go lie down. Far away the black freight train hooted. "She'll be comin' round the mountain when she comes," sang my aunt.

When we finally traveled north it was on a long black train. We had a drawing room on the Southern Railway. The trip took two nights and a day. I sat with my legs straight out in front of me and looked out the window. Every once in a while I would push the green plush of the train seat the wrong way — dark-light, dark-light; then I would peer around at my mother. What should I talk to her about? For months I had been with almost no one but Nanny.

2

Every Sunday the two of us would dress to go to Mass. Under the tent of her white cotton nightgown Nanny would mysteriously draw on first her underclothes, then her long, best silk stockings. Then over the top went her best striped silk dress, and the nightgown fell down in a little puddle at her feet. She fastened the neck of the dress with a cameo brooch, slipping the medal and gold cross inside. Then she would dress me. Daddy would drop us off on his way to his own church, where he was a vestryman. By this time I had a medal of my own — St. Teresa, carrying a sheaf of roses. The Little Flower was Nanny's special saint. That was her middle name, Teresa, after Bessie. Nanny had said I could have St. Teresa for my special saint, too.

Out of respect for St. Paul, Nanny always wore a dark, short-brimmed felt hat which she pulled down almost to the tops of her fiercely blue eyes. I had to wear a bonnet with a snap under the chin that scratched. At the door of the church she would dip her fingers in the scalloped shell over my head and cross my forehead with holy water. The water dropping into the stone shell made a pleasant tinkling sound.

I loved the inside of that church. It was large and dark, like a cave, and you couldn't say anything, but still it was always warm with the rustle of skirts and prayer-book pages and the low groans of old men getting up off their knees. As Nanny leaned forward to pray, I would look up at the reds and blues of the stained-glass windows or try to find through the rows of bodies the pink dress of the plaster saint stretching out her hand from the side aisle. Then the priest would start to chant, little bells would ring, and the church would fill up with the smells of all the different people and the stuffy, interesting smell of incense shaken out by a boy. Above me Nanny's profile was stern but not angry, and I knew she was praying for her brothers and sisters at home, for her father who never made more than two pounds ten a week, and also for the young man she had come over to this country to meet. He had paid her way out, but as soon as she saw him standing on the dock she knew they could never marry. So she went back to being a nanny. The priest in his gold or green or purple cape lifted his hands to the sky. Before him on the altar was a large gold cross. At home we had a black cross with a twisted Jesus hanging over the bed where we slept; there were nails through His feet and the blood ran down, and on His head was the crown of thorns.

One day the side aisle was crowded with children. Their mothers were trying to line them up two by two and making shushing noises. The boys had on dark blue suits, some even wore long pants, but I couldn't take my eyes off the girls. They were dressed in white, like little brides, and on their heads were white veils fastened with wreaths of daisies or wax orange blossoms. Each one carried a bouquet in a white paper ruffle just like a real bride. Nanny had a friend in Greenoch who became a nun — bride of Christ, she called her. Were these the brides of Christ? "Wouldn't you like to make your first Communion?"

whispered Nanny. "But you have to be seven. The age of reason," she added practically.

Nanny took the hairbrush to me. "This hurts me more than it does you," she was almost crying. I had been standing by the ironing board. "Go to the bathroom, Jane," she said. But I wouldn't go. And then I couldn't hold it in any longer, shameful and brown it poured down my legs. The hairbrush hissed through the air. I got down off the bed again stiffly.

I hated Abraham. *Dis*obedient! proclaimed Nanny. But was it Abraham's fault or God's? How could God ask Abraham to kill his only son if He loved him? And how could God let His own Son die? I stared and stared at the twisted Jesus hanging over Nanny's side of the bed. There were nails through His hands, too.

In Isabel's room hung the picture of Paradise. Little boys and girls in yellow and red and blue dresses were standing holding flowers, while lambs and rabbits and sparrows played about their feet. "He prayeth best who loveth best," Isabel read to me from the borders, "All things both great and small." On Pen's wall was the face of a tiger, coming out from among reeds at a water hole in Africa. I never went into Pen's room now if I could help it.

My sins were crying, lying and not wanting to go to the bathroom. "Don't touch yourself, Jane," Nanny pursed up her lips in disgust. One day she said to me, "If you don't stop touching yourself, we'll have to take you to the hospital and get it cut off." I screamed with terror. For a long time I wouldn't stop screaming. Nanny still had all her own teeth. And she had a right to feel proud of them, they were so white. "Soot and salt," she declared — who could afford toothpaste? Their father had taught them all to reach right up the chimney. I watched her smile in fascination. How could anything so white come from anything so dirty as the fireplace? Was this what the priest meant when he said our sins would be washed whiter than snow?

Nanny went up to Communion. She always did that, leaving me alone in the dark wooden pew. But today I felt tired. The people shuffling back down the aisles seemed farther away than usual; the murmur of their prayers was like the sound of the river out our dark bedroom windows on a still winter's night. Nanny was bending over me. My face was cold with sweat. "You fainted," she said with concern. I was surprised to find myself lying in the pew as if it was our bed; a man's jacket lay across my knees. "Poor wee lamb." Daddy came to fetch us, looking worried. Tenderly she carried me out to the car. But after that I couldn't go to church any more, I could only have the Bible stories at bedtime.

"Jane, Jane, Go to Spain, And never come home again!" they chanted at a birthday party. But would I go to Heaven or Hell? I felt very tired. I was standing beside the table where the others were already eating their ice cream and angel food cake. At my place was a bowl of curds.

It was the Depression. But fortunately Nanny's mother had always been a good manager. When nobody else ate liver, she got it off the butcher for dog scraps and they all made a good meal. Not one of them had ever missed a day at school or on the job because of illness. With relish Nanny told how her older sister lost her first post in the hat department in Glasgow. "What you need, madam," Agnes talked back to the customer, "is not a new hat, it's a new face."

Even though it was the Depression, we could still have our new Easter dresses. Mine was to be yellow, with baskets of flowers on a white path down the front. But to wear it, I had to get through the Crucifixion. "Away in a manger, No crib for His bed," we had sung at Christmastime. Now Jesus was the Lamb of God caught by His horns in the bushes. He was betrayed and whipped and they mocked Him and hung Him on the cross saying, "This is the King of the Jews." And they gave Him vinegar to drink. And after He was dead one of the soldiers pierced His side with a spear, and blood and water ran out. And doubting St. Thomas had to thrust his hand into Our Lord's side to make sure He was risen. How could he do that?

All during Lent we read these stories about Jesus. Nanny had no use for people who gave up things for Lent, like my grandmother. When you were really poor, she said, what was left to give up? It was better to show devotion.

I woke up crying. Nanny fussed a bit but brought the water. Then she climbed back into bed and turned her shoulder on me, so as to get back to sleep. I watched the white mound of her body in the thin crack of light from the bathroom door and listened to the slap-slap of the river against the pilings below the house. How could God let His only Son die? And how could Jesus, if He loved me, possibly let me die and go to Hell? After all I was only a child. I tried not to think of the face of the tiger gleaming through the dark from Pen's wall. At any moment he might bare his fangs. Other little animals came down to the water hole, Pen said, and the tiger lay in wait for them.

But suppose there was no Hell? How could God send anybody to Hell if He loved them? Jesus even loved the thief on the next cross. I was almost asleep now. I decided God couldn't have created Hell, there was no room for it.

On Easter morning the sun shone beautifully. Isabel and Pen and I put on our new clothes and were driven through the white streets to our grandparents' house for the big Easter dinner. "Like a picked chicken," one of the uncles said, seeing me in my yellow dress. But Nanny told me I looked a picture. Seated on the high cushion facing my glass of protein milk, I felt high and far away above the rest of the table. The sun shone in on the colors of their new dresses and newly washed hair. Jesus loved me. But today it hardly mattered. For if everybody bad and good went to Heaven, what was the point of being good? There was no Heaven. You died, and that was that.

3

"Take her north to a doctor you can trust. She's dying, and you're dying watching her." That's the way my mother told the story to my aunt, after my father brought home the first real cash he'd been paid in over a year and laid it on the dresser. Never had he worked so hard, complained my mother, but it was because everybody was going bankrupt. We were in Schwartz's toy store. I couldn't make up my mind between a doll with a whole trunk full of clothes and a cardboard village that had a church, a town hall with a star over the front door, a castle, and a lot of horses, sheep and pigs. Finally my mother said I could keep them both. I couldn't believe it. At home we almost never had new toys. Back in the hotel bedroom she helped me pile up the pillows to make snow-capped mountains. On the top peak stood the castle, down below was the church, and on the green blankets over my knees I arranged the little cardboard houses where people really lived, which I liked best of all. But I still couldn't think what to talk to her about. There were three men and three women in that village. One of the women had no hair and a very red face. She looked bossy, and I decided she had no children of her own. She could take care of the pigs.

The nurse in the waiting room called me "she," though I was standing right there. "But she didn't cry," the nurse kept saying stubbornly to my mother, turning the white-rimmed barium glass round and round in her fingers. "Are you sure you didn't just pour it out? They always cry."

He was not stooping or kneeling down to be at my level. Instead he had put his large square hands under my naked armpits and lifted me up to stand on the examining table. From where I stood I could look directly into his blue eyes. He had white curls all over his head, and I thought that was why he was called Dr. Kerley. Naked, I regarded him with trust. "You know," he said at once, "you're going to be all right." How could he understand all that I had felt? He told me before he told my mother.

4

My mother didn't want to leave me alone on the ward but I was delighted. Every day while we shared the small room at the hospital I would creep down to the end of the hall and peer in at the ward door and wonder about the children who lived there. Those children were old campaigners. They could tell the names of the various diseases and how they affected you. Frances, for instance, was an epileptic. That meant you fell down in fits. Frances was very pretty, and I used to love to lie and watch her still profile through the thin cheesecloth curtain that at rest hour divided our two cots. She had long, pale braids, and when she sat up they slid silkily down her back. Frances was almost nine and rarely smiled. After a while I decided she would not get better. You could usually tell.

For over a year I had weighed 42 pounds. Because of the diet my second teeth might not come in with enamel. But I didn't have celiac disease, all I had to do was stay in the hospital and learn how to eat again. Dr. Kerley stood at the foot of my cot, my mother was perched on the side. But I wouldn't look up. I was holding the brimming spoonful so that it sparkled under the bedside bulb. It was my first real supper — cornflakes, with sweet, thin cow's milk.

The nurses on our ward never felt sorry for anyone. That was what was grand about them, they treated us just like ordinary children. Every morning at 6:30 they would wake us by switching on the harsh overhead lights and wiping our faces with grainy washcloths soaked in cold water. Then we had to wait a long time before they brought up breakfast. "Happy birthday, Jane!" announced the chief nurse, setting down across my knees with a thump a tray that had a green cardboard cake on it. Out of the cake came a sunburst of yellow ribbons, and at the end of each ribbon was a small green box. At last I was six. I turned my shoulder on the rest of the ward. Secretly I opened the first box. Inside was a tiny wooden tea set with red trim. As I balanced the long line of cups and plates down the longer line of my sheeted leg, I pretended they were overflowing with chocolate ice cream, cornflakes and angel food. That night I asked the nurse please to tie up all my presents again, so I could have the same birthday tomorrow morning.

The baby with tubes lay on one side of the hall door and Billy was on the other. They were the youngest children on the ward. Billy was only two and a half. The baby slept most of the time, and the tubes curled out from under his white knitted crib blanket and fell in a red garland to the floor. It was rumored he had kidney trouble. My cot was in the far corner, safe between Frances and the wall.

Once a week we were taken up on the roof to listen to stories. There we would be joined by groups of children from other wards, and crippled children would be wheeled in by their nurses in special chairs or carried on portable beds. It was sunny and crisp on the roof, and as you stepped out of the elevator you could see a great sweep of sky, blocks of apartment buildings with a few trees down below, and in the distance the glittering river that was still not as wide as our own river at home in Jacksonville. The storyteller wore a long, flowing robe and had an unusually sweet voice, and we would all sit or lie or stand listening while she recited fairy tales and sometimes sea gulls or a pigeon flew by overhead. My favorite was Boots and His Brothers, where the third child that everyone thinks is stupid grows up to win the princess by kindness or good luck.

One day when we came down off the roof and were crowding through the ward door, we discovered the baby had been taken away. His crib looked flat and white, and the bunch of red tubing was gone from underneath. "Gone for an operation," said the brisk young nurse who was folding his crib blanket. But he never came back. We all knew he must have died, though someone argued he could just have been put in a private room because he was so sick. Soon his place was taken by a cheerful girl with one leg in traction. They had run out of bed space in the bone and joint pavilion downstairs.

"Nurse-ah. Nurse-ah. Nurse-ah." The whole place smelt like a zoo. There was the smell of fear, the warm animal smell of sleeping bodies, and the sharp stink of hospital disinfectant coming up from the floor and the sheets. Billy had started it. He had waked up wanting the nurse and no one was on duty. She must just have stepped down the hall. By the time I woke up, everybody was shouting or crying. The ward was almost dark, and it took me a few moments to make out Billy clinging to the bars of his crib and beating on the top rail with his fist. Billy couldn't talk clearly yet and he was shrieking in panic. Nobody could get over the bars of their own beds to help him. I sat up, then I stood and leaned over the high end of my bed and kicked at the bottom railing with my bare foot. We all began to pound the rails with our hands. The smell grew heavier. Gradually a rhythm was pounded out, and together we began to shout as loud as we could for Billy: "*Nurse*-ah! *Nurse*-ah! *Nurse*-ah!" At last we could see flashlights coming down the hall, sending slanted shadows toward the ceiling as they got closer. Then the overhead lights glared on, and three nurses started fussing through the ward, telling the children to lie down and tucking us in with strict tightness. One of them picked up Billy, who was soaked through. Almost at once he fell asleep with his head on her shoulder. But I couldn't sleep for a long time, thinking of how we had all called together to save Billy.

I fell in love with George. George was a tall, well-built boy of seven, with a fleshy jaw and brown hair that started straight up from his forehead. All that was wrong with him was that he was waiting for another operation on his harelip. We were two of the well ones now, and every day we spent a lot of time together on the sun porch, building towers out of blocks, eating jello at a low table, or chasing each other around the room. "Be quiet, Jane. Now do be quiet, George," the nurses had to say, as we laughed and scuffled. Once they even had to separate us while we were wrestling, pulling George off from on top of me by the back of his blue shirt collar. Another day George was sitting in the big red fire engine pedaling hard and I was sitting on the back and he drove straight through the ward where our cots were and out the door to the hall and ran into the legs of Dr. Kerley. We ricocheted off the wall then, and both of us fell out laughing. When my mother came to visit, she was shocked to find I had learned to talk just like George. That was harelip language. There were hardly any consonants, only animal noises, and the lilt of true sentences running up and down George and I always talked that way. It was our secret code to fool the nurses

It was getting cold. Soon it would be time to go home. My mother came to visit, bringing with her a pair of brown leather leggings outgrown by my northern cousins. She got permission to take me for a walk outside the hospital, and together we set off down the strange city streets. At home I was used to grass and trees, so I stared at the gray, flashing pavements. Then I was leaning against an iron railing, looking down on ranks of boys in gray uniforms who marched and gestured rapidly with their hands. My mother kneeled down next to me and took my body in her arms. "They're deaf and dumb boys, darling," she said. "It's the deaf and dumb school. Those poor boys can't hear anything, and so they have to learn to talk with their fingers." I examined her face in surprise. Her eyes had blurred with tears. Then I pulled away a little and slipped one hand out of its glove, experimentally. It certainly was a cold day not to be able to wear gloves. I looked down at the boys again where they wheeled and beckoned without a sound from across their paved field. But didn't she know we all had something?

IV.
VOCATION:
A LIFE

The Winter Road

. . . they have passed into the world as
abstractions, no one seeing what they are
—Georgia O'Keeffe, 1887-1986

1

Late winter light

Suppose it comes from the snow
blowing all day across your winter road
umber with violet shadows

Or suppose it comes from some energy farther away
that may never be understood
to keep us from repetition
from reciting the litany of loss

The last uncoupling of the galaxies —
how can that be understood?

You stand on a ridge facing silence
You lift your brush

2

Curve of an arm
Ripple of muscles down extended back
Rib cage of cliffs

The eye lays bare the muscle-rows of speech
the prehistoric arteries

It can all be told in color and light and line

Only recompose
the original soft palaver of the earth
        earth red   earth orange   earth purple
        pale Naples yellow   ochres
        even the soft earth greens

Clarify

Or take this "Fragment of the Ranchos de Taos Church," its
Mediterranean statement
        blue of the Isles
        calm butte   archaic thigh

3

Blue
Blue curtains opening on a gray sky
"Black Rock with Blue"
"Sky Above Clouds"

After all men's destruction has been honed away
by the winds that wrap the stars
still there will be blue

Half-blind you go on painting
in a blue smock

And the road past your house
            exaltation of a pear!
carves out the socket
of a hill, then orbits clean off the canvas
bound for *Espanola, Santa Fe and the world*

always there, always going away

tireless calligraphy
on snow without horizon

4

Where I have been
Where I have been is of no importance
To live to be a hundred is of no importance
only *what I have done* with it
　　　　But we love the particular

Where I was born
Where I was born is of no importance
　　　　torn shoe, nursing mouth, patchwork-cushioned chair
　　　　still rocking quietly in the light wind
　　　　of a late summer evening of some life

Nor *how I have lived*
with a handful of rocks
a wooden bodhisattva in a niche
a black door
and the continuous great adventure of the sky

Only what I have made of it
what I have been able to finish
To live to be a hundred is of no importance
This landscape is not human
I was meant to take nothing away

Vocation: A Life

Suite Based on Four Words from Willa Cather

1. DESIRE

. . . too strong to stop, too sweet to lose . . .
(THE SONG OF THE LARK)

1915 It begins in indolence
It begins as a secret intelligence rising like a tune,
opening with the pores
It begins in secret
Thea lies on a rock-shelf, face to the sun,
eyelids closed against sun, the sun roaring
through her ears and pores. Before her a *river of . . . air*
drops three hundred feet, behind her the cliff-house
— a tawny hollow — clings like a swallow's nest
The rock is smooth and warm and above all clean

The rock is above all clean
The Ancient People left no wounds in the earth
but a curious aspiration — a carbon stain
on the rock-roof above a cookfire, turkey bones,
the shard of a pot with a serpent's head in red,
a black water jar
where a woman blazed identical pale cliff-houses

A timid, nest-building folk?

No, the swallows live out their lives in a *wash of air*
The rock-shelf holds its heat
long after the vivid canyon has died into night

It begins as survival

Thea has died to her self, she is reborn
only as a vessel. Climbing the water trail
from the base of the canyon, she is *feet and knees and loins,*
a baby hangs to her back, on her head is a jar

57

of *sovereign* water, for healing. In simplest health
like a gold lizard on the rock-face, she climbs, dreams,
wakes in her cave
to the pulse of a tribal drumbeat,
the cicadas' anonymous drone

Everything drops away
and is reborn as energy. Like a spring
the monotonous tune wells in her throat all day
It has *nothing to do with words,* it is not a complaint
but more like the flex of a muscle. She grows young,
she is older than her mothers. Neediness,
neediness: our first speech
water   fire   seeds
throbs and fades on the solitude forever

But the old stream runs away
heartless
geological
sacred
as its idle lights pick out the canyon floor

Thea is only a *guest.* Bathing in her pool
at the foot of the canyon, among rosy and ochre stones,
screened by the cottonwoods' flicker, she is stunned
for a moment, to sculpture, lifting a huge sponge
halfway to her flushed shoulders. Here it begins:
With her throat could she . . .? With their jars did they
catch the headlong, *shining . . . element?*
Women coiled the clay, women smoothed the colors. Song
dances on her breath, a ball on a column of air

Now everything takes the curve
of a *desire for action,* of a
brilliancy of motion. She
crouches in the bed of the stream

The shards of ceremony glisten
from that bed
in a crack
of the world

2. ROMANCE

> *Oh, I didn't know anything! . . . But . . .*
> *when I set out from Moonstone . . . , I had*
> *had a rich, romantic past*
>
> — Thea

1909 Down by the Republican or Little Blue
      six boys spend the night on a sandbar
      They build their fire
      on a *new bit of world,* a tiny beach
      where fish and turtle bones
      tell over again the legend of evolution
      It's all a retelling
      in the frank, frontier speech of Nebraska
      of a ghost story by Turgenev
      Only here the boys are talking of Coronado
      not of the water-goblin, how he reached
      this very river maybe, how he died
              always afraid of *dying in a cornfield*
              Red Cloud   Pittsburgh   New York
      simplified by his dream. . . .
      A bobcat leaps, a whooping crane
      screams in this virgin tale
      of mound builders, cliff-dwellers, till the "Enchanted Bluff"
      rears out of a homely, imagined desert
      with all her dead on board

Mesa Encantada!
Your reserve blocks my view like a rock

1893 Who could never forget the summer the corn scorched in the ear
Who could never forget how the immigrant farmers went bankrupt
they were sold up, they took to the roads, they took their own lives
a few went crazy at home
Who wrote by night for a dollar a column and studied by day
in your garish hat, in your too-thin coat
Imperious

Write ordinary life as though it were history
. . . so as to make us dream

But one must have simple tastes — to give up a good salary

What it must have cost you, in your red-embroidered Liberty gown
Throw all the furniture out of the window!

What it must have cost you
      not, after all, the Seven Golden Cities
      London   Paris   Bayreuth
      but the past in a crack of the past

Walnut Canyon, Arizona, spring of 1912

for I shall be the first, if I live,
to bring the Muse into my country

Dreamer, you were almost forty
when you finally saw the Southwest

1918 It was always there
Like an old tune out of childhood or country refrain
played over again to four homesick girls
in MY ÁNTONIA, years later, the design was there:

Sandtown   Moonstone   Black Hawk
the failure of Coronado
and the child extravagantly reading
by the star of her railroadman's lantern
at an open window

3. POSSESSION

. . . the design of his life had been the work
of this secondary social man, the lover
— Professor St. Peter

For me the mesa was no longer an adventure
. . . . It was possession
— Tom Outland
(THE PROFESSOR'S HOUSE)

1925 To begin
with the window
as an element of design:
sonata form
Cervantes' tale-within-a-tale
that square open window
giving on the sea
(In the work of the old Dutch masters, though the foreground may be
full
of red-patterned carpets, copper vessels, bedsteads, ripe fruit,
still the girl pouring wine, in the sun, if she looks up
has a map
no, an actual view
of masts "like a forest in winter"
and the steel-gray   wealthy   or is it empty now?
untranslatable sea)

Q. What's left for the mature artist but an examination of method?
A. *It is only the practised hand that can make the natural gesture, — and the practised hand has often to grope its way*

To begin again
in America:
        a *blue, hazy smear*
                the Blue Mesa!
        his *inland sea*
             a *naked blue rock!*
        the Lake
        of the Professor's landlocked childhood
        just glimpsed from his attic
             Tom Outland's
             unsolved landmark
But suppose it is all a mistake

THE PROFESSOR'S HOUSE is a novel about property

Even the Professor's books have been turned into property
        "Histories," he calls them
        History? a
        romance . . . of the imagination! Off the coast of Spain
        once he'd gazed up at the snow-peaks, unfolding rose
        from a matrix of purple water, fading to gold
        toward the West of El Dorado. . . .
        And the design was sound, he could trust it, *it had seen him through*
        He is fifty-two
        with nothing left to write or to love
        but the journal of a poor dead cowhand,
        vibrating and austere
        If words . . . cost money, he thinks,
        they might taste this pure

The Professor as Coronado?

So it wasn't the War
The world broke in two in 1922 or thereabouts
        suicide?
                celibacy?
                        thereabouts?

THE PROFESSOR'S HOUSE is a novel with two heroes
        two possible endings
        two lovers, unacknowledged,
        of the same sex
        a third lover
and in 1923 Isabelle McClung, securely married,
offered you the perfect studio annexed to her French house

He had never learned to live without delight

Even the Professor's women are creatures of property
        not Thea   Alexandra   Ántonia
        classical as jars
        but a "bust" or a "birdcage." The *social . . . bond*
        makes them dressmakers' dummies. To breathe "I love"
        in a world of acquisition, to blurt out "I trust"
        is to lie on a bosom of sawdust
        and fall
                to face a sour wall
                What were you doing on Park Avenue
                in your last apartment, viewless and vast,
                away from the roar?
(In MY ÁNTONIA, how everything swells and subsides quite naturally
in our lost out-of-doors)

THE PROFESSOR'S HOUSE *is . . . the most personal of Willa Cather's novels,* wrote
valiant Edith Lewis; therefore, not autobiographical

unless the light comes from some faraway place
unless the source of light is beyond ourselves
unless we become ourselves
increasingly
The pioneer plot had failed you
In 1923 they gave you the Pulitzer Prize for the wrong book
But weren't you now a famous, indeed a wealthy woman?

What it must have cost you
And this gift of sympathy is [the writer's] *great gift*
to deal, finally, with coldness at heart

sonata form, or
the story of a shipwreck
yet the key changes
as the original theme speaks:

solitary

Whenever Tom enters the mesa he is solitary
Whether from the canyon he looks up, through the falling snow,
to a round red tower, asleep, a city asleep
high on the cliff-face, veiled, in the lavender air
— a cluster of human remains still undisturbed —
or whether he returns just at sunset as the gold dies away
from his plundered birthright, to find it, after all, whole
and the arc of evening sky whole
and the distant stars whole
as they always have been — till now? — he is at home
on earth, alone,
simplified

not possessing but
possessed

4. UNFURNISHING

There was an element of exaggeration in
anything so simple!
(DEATH COMES FOR THE ARCHBISHOP)

1927 Upon this rock
Ácoma
Mont Réal
Upon this rock I shall
scaffolding   sailing
bearing the ghost of the church in its *ship of . . . air*
unburdening
Under the myriad broad galactic stare
Out of this yellow rock
Out of this clay, stuff of the planet's veins
Out of my body I build my
but not to be mistaken for death

Whatever is felt upon the page without being specifically named there, — that, one
might say, is created

1943 So the poor singer with painful, broken wrists,
the rich young fellow whose tongue has been torn out,
reveal one aging writer, her hand in a splint,
unable to dictate
having lost the pure thrust from throat to page

And this is all we know of your last novel, HARD PUNISHMENTS, left unfinished
at your death and destroyed according to your will

Before that, a sort of litany:
OBSCURE DESTINIES
SHADOWS ON THE ROCK
DEATH COMES FOR THE ARCHBISHOP

the gift of tongues
in a clean adobe room
only the shadows
violet . . .

It begins again
as a miracle, that is
a change in perception

I feel as if I had been journeying over the rim of the world
for ten years: October to October
You have *teased* [my] *mind*
and this is *sympathy.* Last night as low gray clouds
drove rapidly across a raw, towering sunset
like the scooped-out wall of a canyon seen from below,
I stood in a meadow near Jaffrey, invoking two crows
to fly from here to the gravesite. Edith lies at your feet
On your stone is chiseled . . . THAT IS HAPPINESS: TO BE DISSOLVED
INTO SOMETHING COMPLETE AND GREAT   The next words
ring only in silence: *When it comes to one, it comes*
as naturally as sleep

When we try to sum up a lifetime, events cease to matter
just as, in the end, a novel's
plot does not matter
What we came away with was never written down
Vibration, overtone, timbre, a fragrance as distinct
as that of an old walled garden . . . *The text is not there —*
but something was there, all the same, some intimacy,
all that is needed
in a vigorous, rich speaking voice

[Your] *secret?*
It is every artist's secret. Your secret
was *passion*

The singer, the professor, the religious
— three motifs I understand —
and the child
But my motifs are not my subject, cried the painter,
my subject is

How the *vehemence of the sun suggested motion!*

1927   Like Don Quijote and Sancho, they are always on the move,
the two padres. The Bishop is alone
in a wilderness of red sand-hills
Or together they slog among the Truchas, lead-purple under rain
Or the Bishop approaches the pueblos, white, ochre, sullen rose,
through a sandstorm, under starlight. He is drowning in snow
but is saved by his young Pecos guide. With his Navajo friend
he is riding through *blue . . . stinging air,*
tossed by the shadows of a cloudscape, monotonous and free

without ownership, without scar
of European conquest or dreams

Here the earth was never a *second body*
but only the *floor of the sky*

*Artistic growth is, more than it is anything else, a refining of the sense of
truthfulness*

glimpse of a dooryard, glimpse of the South:
acacia, with its *intense blue-green . . .*
colour of old paper window-blinds

touch and pass on

The Archbishop forgives himself everything, even his mistakes
were no more than *accidents.* He is outside time
Poverty, solitude
have strangely flowered. And the Indian

will survive — so he consoles himself
He who came with the buffalo has *lived to see*
the railroads . . . dreamed . . . across the mountains
Carnelian-fired hills
reach out to enfold his cathedral   Sangre de Cristo
rock of living gold
incomplete as friendship in action

I shall die of having lived

But nothing can take this away
Not according to my desires, but if it be for thy glory
supreme mirage of the flesh!

gold of a desert morning
light by which the writing
was composed

NOTES

"The Calling"
Direct quotations are from Muriel Rukeyser's poem "The Outer Banks" and THE
AMERICAN HERITAGE DICTIONARY. Reference is also made to an earlier poem,
"Then I Saw What the Calling Was," and to Rukeyser's prose life of the
Elizabethan navigator/explorer/astronomer, THE TRACES OF THOMAS HARIOT.
Of this 350-page work she said (*New York Quarterly,* summer 1972): "The Hariot
book is a footnote to the Outer Banks poem." She changed the last line of "The
Outer Banks" as shown and described it as a breakthrough. On the back cover of
HARIOT is a close-up by Berenice Abbott of part of Rukeyser's eyebrow and one
great eye.

"Hotel de Dream"
Cora Crane, the common-law wife of Stephen Crane, both before and after their
literary life together in England, ran a bawdy house in Jacksonville called Hotel de
Dream.

"Being Southern"
"Einstein *like a disembodied spirit*" — my father's words.

"Seventeen Questions About KING KONG"
I am indebted not only to repeated viewings of the film but also, for general back-
ground information, to THE MAKING OF KING KONG by Orville Goldner and
George E. Turner. I learned about Uncle Farmie's gift of EXPLORATIONS AND
ADVENTURES IN EQUATORIAL AFRICA from Ronald Haver's DAVID O. SELZNICK'S
HOLLYWOOD. The last line of the poem was said to me in conversation.

"Clementene"
Muriel Rukeyser used often to ask groups, from elementary school kids to middle-
aged graduate students, to write a few lines beginning *I could not tell.* In our most
secret conflicts, she believed, lie our inescapable poems.

"How Can I Speak for Her?"
Thanks to my cousin Nancy Osborne Bennett for tracing some of the historical
material mentioned here, and to Judith Gleason for describing the look of certain
Yoruba scarifications and repeating the sounds of the young girls' speech and songs.

"The Winter Road"
All quotations in italics are from GEORGIA O'KEEFFE by Georgia O'Keeffe.
Painting titles are in quotation marks except for "The Winter Road," which is

referred to specifically in Part 3. I am indebted for several details in Part 3 to Eleanor Munro's ORIGINALS: AMERICAN WOMEN PAINTERS.

"Vocation: A Life"

During one October spent in Iowa, I began to reread the works of Willa Cather, and it soon became clear to me that whenever she wrote about the Southwest, she was also writing about art. I have always loved serial paintings, such as Monet's waterlilies, where the same subject is studied again and again under different lights and in different weathers. In Cather's case, whenever she returned in imagination to the mesas and Anasazi cliff-dwellings and clean skies over the desert, it seems she was pondering the mystery of vocation at a different lifetime stage. Thus Thea's sexual awakening in Panther Canyon (Walnut Canyon) in THE SONG OF THE LARK (1915) really marks her determination to go to Germany to become a singer. (Cather "was convinced that the great thing was *desire* in art" — Bennett.) And even before she herself first visited the Southwest — a visit that coincided with her final leave of absence from *McClure's Magazine* in order to write full-time — she had evoked the glowing image of the Mesa Encantada in a story about small-town Nebraska boys, "The Enchanted Bluff" (1909).

In THE PROFESSOR'S HOUSE (1925) Cather again evoked the mesa, this time the Blue Mesa (Mesa Verde), as a sort of window opening out beyond all she most feared from a successful middle age: fame soured by lack of privacy, wealth that is not freedom but a product, sexual crisis, exhaustion of primary subject matter, bankruptcy of the national/colonial dream. (The Professor's eight-volume history is a homage to the Spanish Conquistadors.) BY DEATH COMES FOR THE ARCHBISHOP, written only two years later, we are released wholly into the land-scape, but the landscape has become post-Impressionist, valedictory. The struggle is no longer in the present.

"Write ordinary life as though it were history . . . so as to make us dream" is my amalgam, freely translated, of two quotations from Flaubert that hung over the desk of Cather's friend and mentor, Sarah Orne Jewett. In a memorable letter of December 1908, Jewett counseled the younger woman: "The writer is the only artist who must be a solitary and yet needs the widest outlook upon the world." "For I shall be the first . . . to bring the Muse into my country" is of course Cather's own rendering of Virgil's lines from MY ÁNTONIA.

All other quotations are from works by or about Willa Cather — besides those already mentioned, A LOST LADY and Cather's essays in NOT UNDER FORTY and WILLA CATHER ON WRITING; also THE WORLD OF WILLA CATHER by Mildred R. Bennett, WILLA CATHER LIVING: A PERSONAL RECORD by Edith Lewis, and WILLA CATHER, A MEMOIR by Elizabeth Shepley Sergeant.

ACKNOWLEDGMENTS

My thanks to the editors of the following magazines, where many of these pieces first appeared, sometimes in slightly different versions:

The American Poetry Review: "The Calling," "The Green Notebook," "The Infusion Room," "Ordinary Detail," "The Past," "Wanda's Blues"

The American Voice: "Hotel de Dream"

Antaeus: "Bloodroot"

Aphra: "Childhood in Jacksonville, Florida"

Global City Review: "Being Southern"

The Iowa Review: "The Children's Ward," "Class," "Estrangement," "Long, Disconsolate Lines"

The Kenyon Review: "Clementene," "From the Journal Concerning My Father," "How Can I Speak for Her?" "Vocation: A Life"

Nimrod: "My friend," "My Mother in Three Acts"

The Paris Review: "Seventeen Questions About KING KONG"

Also: "What the Seer Said" originally appeared in *The New Yorker.* "The Winter Road" originally appeared in *Ploughshares,* vol. 15, no. 4. Part 3 of "From the Journal Concerning My Father,"under the title "Flute Song," originally appeared in *Ploughshares,* vol. 8, no. 1; "Flute Song" was reprinted in SCAFFOLDING: SELECTED POEMS. "Long , Disconsolate Lines" was reprinted in THE PUSHCART PRIZE XVI.

In several poems, brief quotations from the works of others have been incorporated in italics. In "Vocation: A Life," particular acknowledgment is due to Alfred A. Knopf, Inc., which first published DEATH COMES FOR THE ARCHBISHOP, FIVE STORIES BY WILLA CATHER, A LOST LADY, NOT UNDER FORTY, THE PROFESSOR'S HOUSE, and WILLA CATHER ON WRITING, all by Willa Cather, and WILLA CATHER LIVING: A PERSONAL RECORD by Edith Lewis.

I am grateful for fellowships from the Bunting Institute of Radcliffe College and the National Endowment for the Arts, and for residencies at Blue Mountain Center, the Wurlitzer Foundation, Yaddo, and most especially the MacDowell Colony, during which much of the work in this book was conceived and written.

It's a pleasure to acknowledge here some of my debt to Charlotte Cunningham-Rundles, M.D., Ph.D., of the Immuno-Therapy Group of the Division of Clinical Immunology at Mt. Sinai Hospital, New York City; to senior clinical research nurses Sarah Martin and Monica Reiter; and to my companions in the Infusion Room, named and unnamed.

And finally, my gratitude always to the friends who have given me clear-sighted criticism and support both imaginative and practical, among them Maggie Anderson, Rachel Cooper Baker, Linda-Ruth Berger, Bobbie Bristol, Martha Collins, Daniel Cooper, Katie Cooper, Beatrix Gates, Padma Hejmadi, Marie Howe, Jan Heller Levi, Cynthia Macdonald, Richard McCann, Robert Nichols, Grace Paley, Nora Paley, Susan Pliner, May Stevens, Jean Valentine, Sally Appleton Weber. Without my long dialogue with Adrienne Rich, the book in its present form would simply not exist.

The following poems have dedications:
    "The Green Notebook" is for May Stevens and Rudolf Baranik;
        "Class" is also for May Stevens
    "My friend" is for and largely by Sylvia Winner
    "The Hobby Lobby" is for Cynthia Macdonald
    "The Past" is for Martha Collins
    "Wanda's Blues" is for Joan Cooper
    "The Winter Road" and "Desire" are for Katie Cooper